Western Steam Days Remembered

Strathwood

Western Steam Days Remembered

Front Cover: An officer of the railway stands aside and affords full respect to 6029 King Edward VIII as the 4-6-0 sweeps majestically into Swindon in 1959. **Strathwood Library Collection**

Strathwood

Western Steam Days Remembered

First published 2013

ISBN 1-905276-42-7
ISBN 978-1-905276-42-4

Published by Strathwood, 9 Boswell Crescent, Inverness, IV2 3ET. Tel 01463 234004
www.strathwood.co.uk

Contents

Page

Preface

Enthusiasm for the first two volumes of Steam Days Remembered has sent me back once again into the archive to make another selection of some of my favourite shots from the fifties and sixties in colour. This time around I have called upon another old friend to puts some words together about his experiences as a younger man growing up with steam. Indeed you will glimpse a few similarities perhaps to your own memories of the time as we venture through this collection together back into a bygone era.

Many readers will be familiar with the name of Peter Coton being acredited to a number of previous releases in the Sixties Spotting Days series. These have been drawn from Peter's collection of colour slides taken at a time when every month the railway periodicals announced a long list of freshly withdrawn locomotives, some old friends, others not seen yet. But what of the man behind the lense, who is this fellow who fortunately for those of us who were perhaps either too young, or too poor as schoolboys at the time, to have the money and equipment to take such shots. Or even be allowed by our parents to venture that far from our home town! As sadly far too many of the older guard of enthusiasts who were active at the time have now passed on, their photographic collections sometimes preserved in a loft somewhere but more often forgotten about or more tragically thrown out after a suitable period of mourning by the family. If you are concerned by this prospect do get in touch, and you could see your favourite shots whether black and white or in colour published in the coming months.

So we should give thanks to Peter and those others who took such shots and have been kind enough to allow us to see their work published today.

Kevin Derrick
Inverness 2013

A society visit to Swindon Works and here to the running shed coded 82C on 24 September 1961 was blessed with warm early autumn sunshine, and respectfully dressed members were allowed to roam free to take their photographs. *Frank Hornby*

6

Introduction — **Go West Young Man**

Good fortune would smile upon 1420 seen at Leominster in March 1961, for preservationists rather than scrap dealers would win her tendering process after being withdrawn in November 1964. **Strathwood Library Collection**

When reminiscing about the past, you hope to strike a chord with others, trigger their memories, invite challenges and stimulate debate. All of these, combined with the evocative illustrations that follow, lead to the seemingly endless fascination with the age of steam amongst those of us old enough to have seen at least some of its glory.

For the first few years after the war, my parents used to holiday in Looe, Cornwall. My first Great Western recollections date from 1950 when my father took me to Paddington, gave the guard 2/6d and asked him to tip me out at Liskeard. I was to spend time with the young son of the owners of the B & B where we stayed. Sixty years later you can wonder at many aspects of that alone - would you despatch a 7 year-old on such a journey on his own today, would the same guard "work through", would I be met at the far end, etc, etc.

I was not yet at the "spotter" stage, but the seeds were being sown. My only real memory of the journey was as the 45xx ran around the B set in the shadow of Moorswater

viaduct. Standing at the open carriage window, I could see that the points were set for the line down to Moorswater shed, yet the clear sound of the loco coming towards me could be heard. In what I suppose was fatal fascination I stood and waited for the inevitable derailment, was amazed that it somehow didn't happen. And so my first experience of spring-operated points was learnt.

It was 5 years later that I noted down my first GW locomotive - 5055 Earl of Eldon at the bufferstops at Paddington. I had finally badgered my parents into getting my first "combined" abc and could now do the job properly ! Like many other lads, I regularly did a circuit of the London termini. My dad had a shop in Tunbridge Wells and he would give me a few shillings and off I'd go. 9.01 'stockbroker's' train with a Schools to Cannon Street, Circle Line to Liverpool Street and the cavernous, sulphurous gloom there; and a regular anti-clockwise circuit to King's Cross, St.Pancras, Euston and Paddington. Ending up at Waterloo main line before going over to Waterloo East and catching the 4.20pm ex Charing Cross back home.

Paddington was always a delight. The locos were almost always clean and most of the tender engines were 'namers'. So the ratio of named 'cops' was always best there. And my next memorable trip was a family holiday to the Isles of Scilly. We took the overnight train, but I declined a sleeper - there was much too much to miss! Details are long forgotten but some images endure. Like the highly burnished Modified Hall

No such luck for 4300 Class Mogul 6381, seen at Hereford with a Gloucester service on 13 July 1963 just before a harsh thunderstorm struck, as it would be withdrawn in November 1963 and scrapped seven months later. **Peter Simmonds**

A recent visit to the nearby works at Swindon has been afforded to one of the Churchward design of 2-8-0s at the turn of the 1960s. Another overhaul would be unlikely before being taken out of traffic in December 1963. *John Gill*

which left on a westbound parcels as folk tried to find their allocated sleeping compartments, and then wedge all their luggage in somehow. Later on, the unmistakeable silhouette of withdrawn Dukedogs at Swindon, awaiting their new career as razor blades. Funereal progress past Bristol and a reacquaintance with the Modified Hall at Taunton which had taken the more direct route via Newbury.

But simply unforgettable, the climb out of Newton Abbot with the sight and sound of two locos attacking Dainton, firehole doors open for a constant feed of fuel for the climb and the orange glow in the inky black of pre-dawn, accompanied by that indescribable music from the chimneys. Tiredness overcoming me and virtually no recall after the Royal Albert bridge for the trip through Cornwall. A year later it was Mullion, involving a change at

Gwinear Road and a trip down the Helston branch, and a further year on, Tenby. That one, beginning to mirror the pattern of post-war prosperity, being undertaken by road, but not denying a trip from Tenby to Pembroke Dock behind 7804 Baydon Manor and the discovery of where Neyland was!

My father was a picture-frame maker and we had an elderly customer, Miss Hithcock, who lived in Bath and would turn out charcoal sketches by the dozen, each of which were uniformly framed in 1 inch flat oak. It was worked out that it was cheaper (and more reliable) for me to carry her framed masterpieces down to Bath than to package them up securely enough to survive transit by any other means. And so it came to pass that I would be able to leave on the trusty 9.01 as the shop opened, get over to Paddington for the "Merchant Venturer", first stop

Bath. Always a tip-top condition Castle turn, its punctuality was exemplary. A quick taxi ride and goods delivered and it was back for the 2.10 stopping at Chippenham only, and this would get me on to the 4.20 from Charing Cross, due at Tunbridge Wells Central at 5.18, 12 minutes before closing time. What a good day's work and it probably accounted for a trip each school holiday until I was no longer eligible for half fares. One reflection of how locos were rostered for the same train, sometimes for months on end, was a homebound run behind 5066 Wardour Castle and the next time around it was the same loco, but renamed Sir Felix Pole.

August 1955, long and hot and no doubt I was an irritating little 12 year old. But my dad had a heart of gold and knew that I was relatively easy to entertain. One particular day he gave me a pound and said "off you go then", and, with riches beyond the dreams of avarice, off I went. You know the first and last legs already, but that particular day I abandoned the circuit of the Circle line and headed straight for Paddington and the "Inter City", complete with a Stafford Road King at the sharp end. One stop at Leamington and there I am in Britain's second city, asking directions for New Street.

It was there I bought my first copy of "Trains Illustrated", with a Lord Nelson on the cover, and the news within that the first LMS Beyer-Garratts had been withdrawn. And whilst I can't recall which royal personage had taken me north, I will never forget my first run with a rebuilt Scot, 46162 Queens Westminster Rifleman. I stood the whole way, stopping at Coventry only and with grit in my eye from Rugby onwards. My dad asked where I had been for the day and I think he was quite proud of my initiative. My mother was horrified!

So as one year blended into the next, the writing was on the wall for steam, but no underlining for 5089 Westminster Abbey, which had remained for years the only one of the 5000 series of Castles that had escaped my gaze.

After the late 50's, when Swindon had achieved so much good work adapting their fleet for the post-war austerities of poorer quality coal and the decline in maintenance

standards, it was bordering on tragic to witness how the proud traditions evaporated. I guess the last stand by Swindon was their championing of hydraulic transmission for their diesel modernisation programme, but as successive Westerns emerged, you could tell the spark had gone and the names bore it out - Western Disaster, Western Points Failure, Western Decline, etc. The glitter went out of the region, and locos were sent out in a condition which would have had shed masters of a few years previous hauled before the management and berated. We now remember the death throes of Western steam, the much loved Brunswick Green which had been lovingly bestowed on almost everything now long buried beneath the muck and grime.

Above: Another visit to the running shed at Swindon on 16 October 1960, this time yields 7824 Iford Manor alongside 4969 Shrugborough Hall. *Frank Hornby*

Left: Now in the last year of it's six year service life was 92220 Evening Star put to work on the Bromford Bridge to Avonmouth Esso fuel train at Coaley Junction on 13 July 1964. *Gilroy Kerr*

On 29 May 1964, three weeks after an epic high-speed run which set off behind 4079, saw a wonderful effort by a Modified Hall as its replacement, with further contributions from Clun Castle and Earl of Ducie, but no 100mph as hoped, I made one of my late pilgrimages to Old Oak Common. My long-time friend John Tiley was with me and shouted to me that there was something I ought to see inside the remaining roundhouse. My search for 5089 was over. She wasn't in the best of shape, working out her time from Oxley shed., and certainly not on class A duties. But the green paint shone through the patina of grime and the thoroughbred lines of the rebuilt Star were plain to see. John and I retired for a celebratory pint in the grotty little pub just up the road on the way to see if there was anything worth pointing a camera at on Willesden that day.

So as 1964 morphed into 1965, Great Western steam finally gave up the ghost. The Kings had long gone and the handful of Castles reflected the attitude that now prevailed - 5042 Winchester Castle bereft of safety valve bonnet and as embarrassing as the thought of your grandmother in the nude. The remaining Halls and Granges, with bare patches on the cabsides where the numberplates had been rudely wrenched off, the spikes of steel that had once held nameplates and the pervading sense of decay and imminent death. Only Clun Castle relieved this awful period and the cancer of the lost spirit now transferred to the diesels, now plastered in an unrelieved all over blue and allowed to get as filthy as the steam they replaced would soon be upon us all.

So in some way, it was almost a relief when the final fires were dropped and Great Western steam was taken out of its misery.

Peter Coton
Essex 2012

On a sunny day in 1965, 4079 Pendennis Castle blows off from the safety valves, as it runs easily on this day along the down relief line at Twyford. **Strathwood Library Collection**

Page opposite: What connoisseur of Western Region steam could walk past the ex-works Castle Class, 7007 Great Western at Swindon on 28 May 1961 with a camera loaded with colour film, and not take an exposure in such lovely sunshine? **Late Norman Browne/Strathwood Library Collection**

A mix of 2-8-0 designs from Riddles and Collett mix it with a selection of Western Region express and mixed traffic 4-6-0s outside in the shed yard at Swindon on 24 September 1961, as society members make their way around 82C under the watchfull eye of the shed foreman. *Frank Hornby*

Page opposite: One of the many 5700 Class pannier tanks built after Nationalisation in 1948 was 9680 built here in Swindon and released to traffic in April 1949. On 13 July 1963 it was finding employment with a Kemble stopping passenger service, with diesel multiple units taking over what services the Beeching cuts left, work for such pannier tanks had all but dried up by December 1965 when 9680 was posted as withdrawn. *Peter Simmonds*

Everyday Swindon

Even the pride of the Western Region, in the shape of 6000 King George V could not be kept spotless in everyday service with a light coating of ash, soot and dust adhering to the paintwork of this fine locomotive as it was moved out into the shed yard for the benefit of photographers. The much prized souvenir bell from the engine's visit to the USA for the celebrations of the centenary of the Baltimore & Ohio Railway in 1927 was always much polished come what may. *Richard Icke*

A closer view of 7824 Iford Manor was also taken by our late cameraman on 16 October 1960. In another two months the Charles Collett designed Manor, which was among the last eight of her class released into traffic during December 1950 would celebrate it's tenth birthday. Withdrawn in November 1964, it would be reduced to scrap by the end of February the following year, what a sad waste of resources by those responsible! *Late Norman Browne/Strathwood Library Collection*

Not exactly clean and prestine for the appearance at the head of what was at one time world's fast train service, the Cheltenham Spa Express which by 1959 the duty has fallen today to be headed by Castle Class, 5084 Reading Abbey as it brings it's rake of chocolate and cream Mark I coaches into the west end of Swindon with the up service. ***Strathwood Library Collection***

Page opposite: Works overhauls were still being undertaken for steam locomotives at Swindon Works on 28 May 1961, albeit alongside the construction of replacement diesel hydraulic Type 4s. The last of the thirty strong County Class designed by Hawksworth to be built, was 1029 County of Worcester put into service in April 1947. This quick 1961 works visit would see the locomotive out until withdrawn late in 1962. ***Frank Hornby***

Rolling stock overhauled at Swindon from the late 1950s would be turned out either in chocolate and cream livery for use on prestige expresses, on the Western Region allocated coaches, or into maroon for other regions as the blood and custard scheme fell out of favour. This view from the time shows 1019 County of Merioneth in very much workaday condition. The county after which it was named was formed in 1284 under the terms of the Statute of Rhuddlan, and once held Dolgellau as it's former county town. *Strathwood Library Collection*

Page opposite: At the time of the County Class's introduction there were twenty Class 5800 0-4-2Ts in service, as the 1950s progressed the class remained intact with many examples still retaining their GWR liveries. By the close of 1957 eleven of the class had been withdrawn that year, as the end of 1959 approached, when this view was taken in the centre roads at Swindon station just 5815 remained in service. Withdrawn in April 1961, it was seen by many visitors to the works dumped out the back with the rest of the scrappers unitl cut up in the summer of 1964. *Strathwood Library Collection*

Locomotives stabled dead in the sidings adjoining Swindon's Gas Works could be awaiting overhaul such as here with 5039 Rhuddlan Castle in August 1959, or for many it would mean something much more sinister as they were destined for cutting up instead! *Late Norman Browne/Strathwood Library Collection*

Page opposite: The first weekend of March 1966 saw four enthusiast specials run over the Somerset & Dorset utilising nine steam locomotives, a Hymek and a DMU. Used on both days was Battle of Britain Class, 34057 Biggin Hill seen here at Evercreech Junction, the line closed the following day. *Tony Butcher*

Sad & Decayed

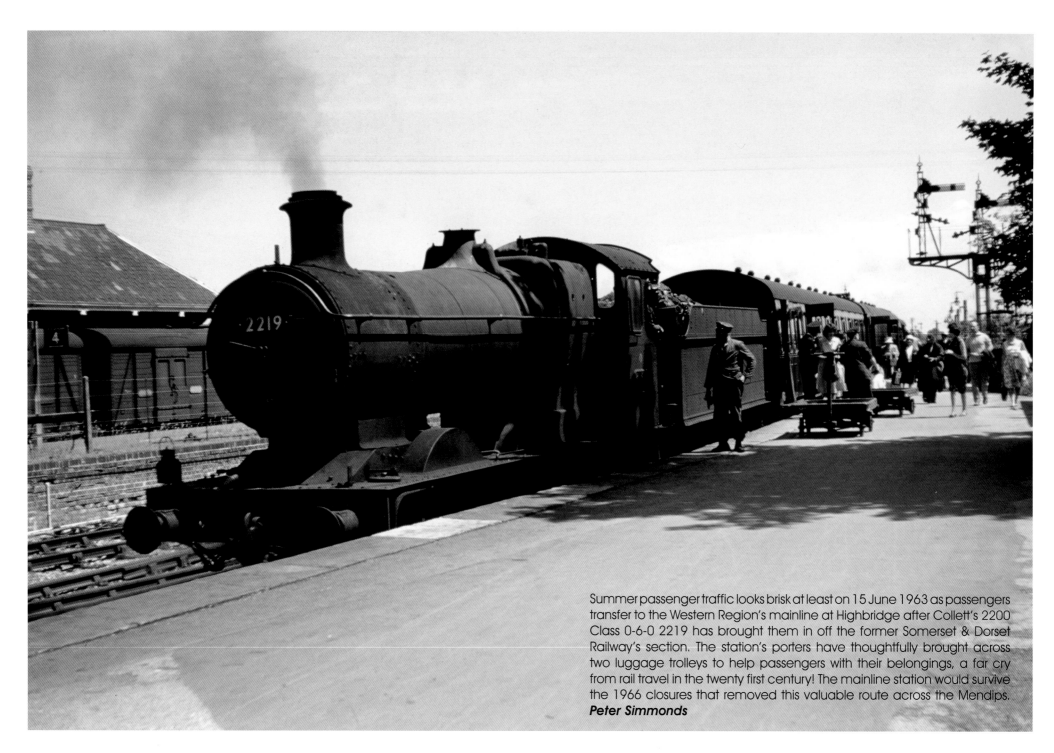

Summer passenger traffic looks brisk at least on 15 June 1963 as passengers transfer to the Western Region's mainline at Highbridge after Collett's 2200 Class 0-6-0 2219 has brought them in off the former Somerset & Dorset Railway's section. The station's porters have thoughtfully brought across two luggage trolleys to help passengers with their belongings, a far cry from rail travel in the twenty first century! The mainline station would survive the 1966 closures that removed this valuable route across the Mendips.
Peter Simmonds

The influx of British Railway's designed Standards from the late fifties had started to push out the designs of the former companies, coupled with the transfer of responsibility between the Southern and Western Regions, saw neither happy to spend resources on the route. Steam percolates into the cold winter air in early 1965 from underneath Standard Class 4MT 80043, as the driver looks back along his rake of Southern coaches whilst he awaits departure of his stopper away from Bath Green Park. *Edward Dorricott*

Staying at Bath's Green Park station, whose roof fortunately survived the line's closure for some more activity with British Railway's Standards, as Class 3MT 82041 readies to depart with the 11.41 service to Bristol Temple Meads on 11 December 1965. Sadly it looks as though the only passengers today may be enthusiasts taking in the line, as it was posted to close as of the year's end. *Douglas Twibbel*

It was only the rival bus company's inability or lack of desire to run the replacement bus service that gave the former Somerset & Dorset Railway's route a short reprieve until the beginning of March 1966. That last winter on the line saw this photograph taken at Evercreech Junction, as one service has just left for Bath whilst Standard Class 4MT, 80041 awaits the road southwards to Bournemouth with a stopper. *Late Ken Pullen/Strathwood Library Collection*

Severn Bore

Page left: One of the large Prairie Class 5101 tanks 4156, leads a Collett Class 2884 2-8-0 out of the Severn Tunnel in 1964 with a lengthy goods, long before the M4 Motorway stole what railway traffic survived the recession of the late 1970s. *Gerald Peacock*

Another cameraman joins us lineside at Caldicot on 17 October 1964, as Standard Class 9F 92228 rolls along nicely with a train of coal empties. *Dave Down*

It appears that the second C in the station's nameboard looks to have split and hangs down appearing to miss-spell Caldicot the following day, as one of the last built of the original Collett designed Hall Class, 6953 Leighton Hall looks pretty weary as it makes its way through with a rake of empties. ***Dave Down***

The lower quadrant home signal shows up well against the sighting board at the Aust Road catch points protecting the Severn Tunnel in 1964 as a pairing of Classes 7200 and 5101 keep their goods train's couplings stretched out. *Gerald Peacock*

Keeping a sharp lookout the fireman catches some fresh air as he hangs over the side of one of the modified 2-8-0s with side window cabs designated 2884 Class as they pass Blaise near Pilning with an up freight with 2896 in charge. *Gerald Peacock*

Page opposite: Another of these robust locomotives has the double peg at Cattybrook again in 1964, with 2891 this time in charge. This would be the last summer for the majority of steam workings through the Severn Tunnel. Through all of the 1950s there were eighty three of these 2884 Class in service to call upon. One was withdrawn during 1962 with further withdrawals during 1963/4 reducing the number of serviceable locomotives to just thirty four by the start of 1965 their last year in traffic. *Gerald Peacock*

Western Rover

Page left: Starting this round up of Western Region locations we begin at Cardiff East Dock on 12 July 1964 for a fine portrait of 92220 Evening Star showing off its unique for Class 9F lined Brunswick Green livery complete with express headlamps. **Strathwood Library Collection**

Next to Pontypool Road on 15 August 1962 as we telephone the signalman for permission to go out on the mainline whilst 6335, 9611, 3682, 3815, 4668 are all in view on this day along with an unknown Class 5600. **Strathwood Library Collection**

Page left: The sun is setting on Gloucester shed coded 85B in August 1964, although it remained open to steam until December 1965 the presence of the diesel invasion is being felt with a newly built Brush Type 4 and a Hymek mingling with the Panniers, Prairies and 4-6-0s. *Win Wall/Strathwood Library Collection*

Doing its best to shroud the shed yard and the turntable at Gloucester Horton Road with it's steam was 5101 Class, 4100 shortly before it was withdrawn in November 1965. *Strathwood Library Collection*

On 13 October 1962 at Neath Riverside we find a pairing of Panniers 3706 and 9796 with a train marking the closure of the old Neath & Brecon route for passenger services. This was the second station at this point opening as the first one closed in 1892, Neath Riverside station finally closed two years later after this view. The South Wales mainline crossed the line here on an overbridge just to the right of the photographer. *Strathwood Library Collection*

It's a meloncholy task for 6931 Aldborough Hall now devoid of its name and numberplates on 31 July 1965, found passing through Cardiff General dragging Panniers 4663, 4639, 4623 and 5600 Class, 5655 which were all posted as withdrawn the previous month and now on their way for scrapping. The much rundown Hall 4-6-0 would itself succumb for the scrap dealer's tenders that October. *Strathwood Library Collection*

A chance for the fireman to get up on the tender and trim his coal before departure from Three Cocks Junction in 1963 onto the Swindon built but Ivatt designed Mogul for the London Midland & Scottish Railway, Class 2MT 46519. The first of this class of one hundred and twenty eight engines went into service from Crewe Works in late 1946, the last example from here leaving the works in June 1950. Darlington Works then chipped in with the next batch, their first leaving the former North Eastern Railway's workshops in June 1951. By the time that Swindon took over construction in late 1952 until March 1953, the approval for newer designs of Standards such as Class 4MT 75006 were being favoured, seen here getting away from Banbury on 23 October 1963. Swindon Works built all eighty of this class of 4-6-0 over a seven year period from 1951.

Strathwood Library Collection & Michael Beeton

Most readers will recall the harsh winter of 1963, the snowy conditions drew out our cameraman to Saunderton that February to record another Swindon built locomotive 48479, again to an LMS design as the Class 8F heaves another rake of coal empties through the Chilterns for a refill, to keep the home fires burning that winter. *John Newman*

Page opposite: Another view of a Standard Class 9F on the Avonmouth to Bromford Bridge Esso fuel train, as the Crewe Works built 92059 captivates the group of young lads gathered on the platform at Coaley Junction on New Year's Day 1965. *Gilroy Kerr*

Next we are off to enjoy the warm sunshine once more at sleepy Much Wenlock, with Class 2MT 41201 rostered today for the pick up in May 1961, passenger services would cease the following year. This charming station was built between 1860 and 1862 and formed part of the Wellington to Craven Arms Railway's route absorbed into the Great Western Railway. *Strathwood Library Collection*

Page opposite: Another favourite location for photographers was the much busier Bristol to Birmingham mainline at the head of the Lickey bank near Blackwell, where at least one spotter has arrived lineside by bicycle on 27 July 1963 to witness the passing of Standard Class 5MT 73094. Notice the smaller calling on arms of the signals for the attentions of the banking engine's crews. *Peter Simmonds*

Page left: A healthy extra shove is being afforded to this goods train up the Lickey incline near Bromsgrove, from Hawksworth Pannier 8418 and Standard Class 9F 92079, the latter had taken over from the Midland Railway's Big Bertha 0-10-0 in the mid 1950s here for banking duties. **Strathwood Library Collection**

Trackside gangers work on as 6026 King John brings the Cambrian Coast Express into Birmingham's Snow Hill station in 1961 oblivious to the hissing of escaping steam at the King's front end. **Strathwood Library Collection**

Passengers would prefer to chat under the awning at Builth Road rather than enjoy today's sunshine as the fireman of Class 8F, 48128 climbs up onto the tender whilst his driver stands ready to let the water flow in 1964. **Strathwood Library Collection**

Page opposite: There is some shunting activity taking place in the shed yard at Worcester on 2 September 1962, as Modified Hall, 7921 Edstone Hall makes its way past one of those distinctive Great Western Railway conical water towers. **Frank Hornby**

Worcester shed was once very proud of its allocation of Castles and looked after them with great care, however by 27 July 1963 standards have slipped as 7023 Penrice Castle shuffles about light engine near the station. **Strathwood Library Collection**

Page opposite: Token cleaning has done nothing but highlight the dirt on 7011 Banbury Castle simmering in Worcester's shed yard on 7 June 1964, the glory days have certainly passed now. **Win Wall/Strathwood Library Collection**

The weeds and wild flowers abound, as the driver of Pannier 8717 sits back and enjoys the sunshine at Berkeley Road before departure to Sharpness the year before the closure of the branch which took place in 1964. *Gerald Peacock*

The Great Western's early solution to lightly used branch lines was to introduce diesel railcars, such as this example at Bewdley on 29 August 1959, where it seems a few passengers are looking to board this service along the Severn Valley. These were the days when even older lads were happy to wear shorts and long socks in the summer months. *Frank Hornby*

London Division

At a time when the Modernisation Plan was proposing large fleets of diesel multiple units, to take over duties such as this suburban service arriving at Paddington from Reading and Slough in 1955, behind large Prairie 6106 at the head of a rake of red compartment local stock. *Strathwood Library Collection*

Among the headline early duties for the very last of the British Railways Standard Class 9F's 92220 Evening Star, was on the down Capitals United Express leaving Paddington at 15.55 for Cardiff on 1 July 1960. At this point the famous last built steam locomotive was just over three months into it's short service career. *Douglas Twibell*

The fireman is busy raking forward what's left of his coal supply onboard 7928 Wolf Hall. The penultimate built of the class of seventy one Modified Halls had begun service in October 1950, by 1964 it still looked clean at least when caught alongside a Hymek at the buffer stops at Paddington. *Strathwood Library Collection*

Clearly just ex-works from Swindon was 6016 King Edward V when photographed on the ash pits at Old Oak Common on 12 November 1961, this overhaul would only have to last until September the following year with all of its classmates out of traffic soon afterwards. **Strathwood Library Collection**

Page left: More and more diesels were invading Old Oak Common's roundhouses every month by the time of this shot in July 1963, the working conditions inside these sheds were far superior to many elsewhere. **Win Wall/Strathwood Library collection**

The rebuilding of the facilities at Old Oak Common had already begun with the offices by the time of this view of 6842 Nunhold Grange on 15 March 1959. **Strathwood Library Collection**

A large double sided coaling stage with an equally impressive water tank above it dominated the southern side of the shed yard at Old Oak Common, this ample capacity would be tested at times to keep up with the appetite of not just Castle Class, 5061 Earl of Birkenhead alongside on 20 September 1959, but also to a massive fleet of Panniers, Prairies, 2-8-0s as well as all those fine named copper capped 4-6-0s. **Frank Hornby**

Another of the double chimney fitted Castles built nine years after the example opposite, was 7010 Avondale Castle which acquired its new chimney and draughting arrangement only in November 1960. Built in 1948 this was one of thirty-one Castles to emerge from Swindon Works in the reign of British Railways. *Strathwood Library Collection*

Page left: Before we take our leave of Old Oak Common, how about another viewing back inside the roundhouses on 21 September 1964 to track down 92220 Evening Star once again. *Dave Down*

Heading west along the mainline we arrive at 81C Southall in 1962, to find a far from clean 4976 Warfield Hall being made ready to head a fitted freight westwards. *Strathwood Library Collection*

Some artisitc wag has adorned the last built of the Collett Halls, 6958 Oxburgh Hall with a set of eyes as it moves slowly off shed early one morning in the cool winter sunshine at 81D Reading in 1964, the Western Region shed would close to steam on 3 January 1965 whilst the nearby Southern shed had closed beforehand on 6 April 1964. **Bob Treacher/Alton Model Centre**

The driver of 5042 Winchester Castle has elected to keep his coat on, whilst his younger fireman no doubt having been much more energetic with his firing and preparation duties on this cold morning at Reading shed in 1964, is satisfied with his bib and braces. **Bob Treacher/Alton Model Centre**

Shunting some empty stock around the sidings adjoining the station at Didcot, keeps 4300 Class Mogul 6304 occupied on this occasion in 1959. Built at Swindon Works in late 1920 this locomotive gave good service over a forty-three year period. Two hundred and twenty of these machines joined British Railways in 1948, and they were withdrawn from traffic gradually with one hundred and thirteen examples still on the books at the end of 1961. Their numbers would half again in the next year, once more again in both 1962 and 1963, the last going in 1964 including 6304. **Strathwood Library Collection**

Standing on the down platform at Oxford on 22 April 1959 we can look across to see the driver of Castle Class, 5071 Spitfire taking the opportunity for another oil around before they set off once more. It should be noted this locomotive was one of the batch of Castles built in 1938, when it was named Clifford Castle. In September 1940, it was the first one of twelve of the class to have their names replaced with those of British aircraft familiar to the public during wartime. This fine locomotive which would have been a great preservation candidate was cut up by Cooper's Metals at Sharpness in May 1964. *Frank Hornby*

West Country Wanderings

Page left: A pleasing attempt at trying to keep the black livery clean on large Prairie 6128, well beyond the lifespan of this paint scheme as most of its classmates adopted either lined green or even plain green before they were withdrawn. This was the scene at Oxford in 1962 at a time when only five of the original seventy class members had been withdrawn. *Strathwood Library Collection*

The Western Region once had to share the spoils with the Southern Region or indeed the costs of running services around the West Country. One of the many locations where they met with services, was here at Barnstaple Junction, where 7304 from the 4300 Class stands with a Taunton train on 22 June 1963. *Peter Simmonds*

Page left: Having alighted from our train at Taunton we are in time to see the passage of The Devonian before it was handed over to Warship diesels, although on this day in 1959 it is a scruffy looking 4914 Cranmore Hall in charge. *Strathwood Library Collection*

Surely the use of 1400 Class 0-4-2Ts such as 1451 captured at Tiverton using autocoaches was a most practical way of running shuttle or branch line services, this service was certainly threatened when recorded on 22 June 1963, as the following summer the plucky little locomotive was no more. *Peter Simmonds*

Page left: A much cleaner example is the subject of our next photograph taken four years earlier in June 1959, with 1468 being prepared for service today at Exeter St.Davids, the presence of the diesel shunter in the background has already made some steam duties redundant. *Alan Pike OBE*

Taken the same day was this shot of Standard Class 9F, 92204 moving slowly past 83C Exeter shed. The tender alone weighs nearly fourteen tons more than the slightly built 1400 Class seen opposite, with the Class 9F locomotive itself packing almost another eighty-seven tons. *Alan Pike OBE*

Continueing our journey westwards to Newton Abbot we find a dedicated Royal Mail sorting van tucked in behind 6921 Borwick Hall as the guard stands alongside the cab, no doubt to assist in checking everything was ready for departure with the assistance of the platform's porters, such was the way of life in the summer of 1959. *Alan Pike OBE*

A trip along the branch to Kingswear the previous year on 21 July, yeilds more coaching stock in the rather attractive blood and custard paint scheme, as 4940 Ludford Hall draws in. This locomoive was built at Swindon in the early summer of 1929, it would unfortunately be withdrawn before the dawn of the 1960s being taken out of traffic in November 1959 and cut up the following month. *Strathwood Library Collection*

Back to our summer holidays once more as we spend some time with the family on the beach at Coryton Cove on 20 July 1961, and our attention at least is drawn towards the exhaust of the passing Grange Class 4-6-0 heading westwards no doubt with more holiday makers and day trippers onboard. *Alan Pike OBE*

Okay let's get into the holiday spirit and take a boat trip around the cove at Dawlish as its a nice day in the summer of 1959. The arrival of DMUs has yet to send the use of Prairie tanks on the local services into history and we can take this lovely shot as a fond reminder of the day. *Alan Pike OBE*

Page left: Many enthusiasts were attracted to the branch to Hemyock for the picturesque nature of the stations, and the use of mixed trains transferring the milk tankers to and from the dairy just past the terminus. In the last summer of steam operation in 1963 we find 1421 on duty for today's shunting at the dairy. **Strathwood Library Collection**

On 2 May 1959 there were very few diesel hydraulics available for the mainline services through Plymouth North Road, so it would appear that 6824 Ashley Grange may well have a good few years life left in her on that day. Indeed the first casualty within the eighty strong class would only come in 1960, just nine had fallen by the end of 1963, but the next two years would send everyone of them to the scrapyard. **Frank Hornby**

Plymouth was also a regular host to Southern Region types, not just on the metals of the former London & South Western Railway but also at the city's Laira shed where N Class, 31843 was catching the winter sunshine by the coaling stage on 14 December 1963, with very little signs of her lined black livery showing through the muck. *Dave Down*

Page opposite: On 3 May 1964, West Country Class 34002 Salisbury brings The Cornubian special off the Saltash Bridge, and into the station. This RCTS and Plymouth Railway Circle tour was run to mark the passing of steam on the Cornish mainline. Even with a relatively light load 34002's running was impressive, the Plymouth crew were pleased by the performance of their first and most likely only run with such a Pacific. *Dave Down*

A delightful shot of the Saltash rail motor from Plymouth in May 1959 in the hands of one the 6400 Class Panniers, these were used before the service went over to DMU working on 13 June 1960. *Strathwood Library Collection*

Page opposite: It's an overcast day on 7 June 1961 in the sidings at Looe, and 4575 Class Prairie Tank 5518 certainly doesn't have a lot to handle today. Fortunately the branch survives on passenger revenue alone these days. *Phil Nunn Collection*

We are two hundred and ninety-nine miles from the bufferstops at Paddington, on the platforms here at St.Erth in September 1959, as 1002 County of Berks makes an early stop in its long journey towards the Capital from Penzance. *Late Norman Browne/Strathwood Library Collection*

On 31 July 1965, The Swansea Railway Circle ran their Rambling 56 special behind 5600 Class, 6643 which operated throughout on a tour of the valleys, as here at the now closed Taff & Bargoed Joint Railway station at Bedlinog. *Strathwood Library Collection*

Specials

Page left: The Railway Enthusiasts Club arranged a brake van tour around the Wrexham area on 17 July 1965 hauled by 4683, they called their train The Flintstone Special. *Chris Forest*

Whilst on the SLS arranged Severn & Wye District Tour of 13 May 1961, passenger comfort was much improved with three autocoaches utilising two Panniers, 6437 and 8701 seen here at Coleford. *Strathwood Library Collection*

As can be seen in this view of the special the same day, the auto fitted 6437 was utilised within the auto-coaches, as the ensemble passed the Northern United Colliery in the Forest of Dean at around three thirty in the afternoon, the tour started and finished at Gloucester Central. **Strathwood Library Collection**

The LCGB arranged The Western Ranger Tour on 15 August 1965, interestingly this ran out and back from the Southern Region's Waterloo terminus. After taking in Swindon Works behind 3863, which had taken over from 75066 at Reading General, the batten was handed over here at Radley to 9773 for the train to take a run around the Oxfordshire branches. **Strathwood Library Collection**

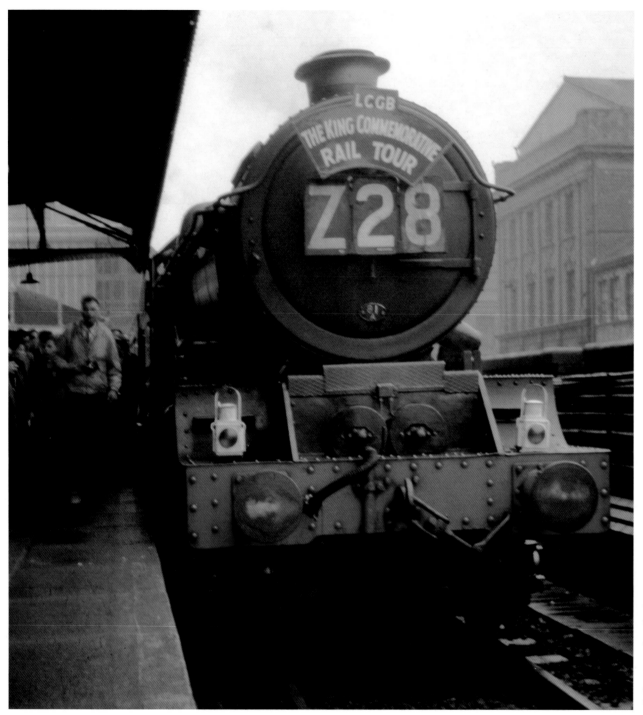

The weather was suitably miserable for the LCGB's The King Commerative Rail Tour which was run on 17 November 1962, behind 6018 King Henry VI seen here at Birmingham Snow Hill. The outward route was from Paddington via Princes Risborough behind the King to Wolverhampton Low Level. Waiting here was 6631 was waiting to take the tour onwards to Leamington Spa where a change to one of Collett's 0-6-0s, 2210 took the passengers back to London Marylebone across country to gain the former Great Central mainline. **Late Vincent Heckford/Strathwood Library Collection**

Page opposite: Another interesting trip was undertaken behind 7029 Clun Castle on 3 April 1965, starting from Birmingham Snow Hill with a run towards London via High Wycombe to take the Greenford curve, and back towards Maidenhead where this stop was made before heading for Swindon Works. After the works visit the tour participants entrained once more behind the Castle towards Didcot for the curve taking them back northwards to Oxford and on to Kings Norton, where steam was exchanged for D5226 to take the run under the wires into New Street. **Edward Dorricott**

Enthusiasts tours in the early 1960s were so interesting, as they were arranged to take in as many threatened routes as they could with as many surviving steam locomotive types as they could conjour up. One such example was with the LCGB's, The Thames, Avon and Severn Rail Tour on 12 October 1963, we see it here at Stratford Old Town with 6368 and 2246 in charge, but 7005 Sir Edward Elgar, the preserved T9 120, 31790, 45552 Silver Jubilee, 82023 and 92223 all did their bit on the day. *Strathwood Library Collection*

But some tours just could not be run with the luxury of such motive power due to weight restrictions, as here near Princess Royal Colliery in the Forest of Dean on 20 June 1964. Tour participants enjoyed a wide ranging tour of these freight routes in brake vans instead, hauled behind both 1658 and 1664 seen here. The tour was called the Severn Boar II and was a repeat running of the same tour a fortnight earlier, such was the demand for tickets. *Strathwood Library Collection*

The two favoured Castles 4079 Pendennis Castle and 7029 Clun Castle, were much used at this time for enthusiasts specials. Such as here with the former at the head of an Ian Allan jaunt from Paddington to Worcester and back via both the Oxford and Swindon routes on 8 August 1965. Then to commemorate the Farewell to Steam on the Western Region on 27 November 1965, it was Clun Castle that was selected. We see it at Bristol Temple Meads, but D1006 Western Stalwart and D6881 with D6882 ran legs as well unfortunately. It seems several parents took their offspring to witness what might have been their last glimpse of a live steam engine that day. *Both: Strathwood Library Collection*

Thankfully it was not the end of Western steam on the mainlines as two specials were run on 4 March 1967, when Ian Allan arranged for The Birkenhead Flyer with 4079 Pendennis Castle and 7029 Clun Castle with The Zulu. Both specials are seen here at Chester whilst the trains went on to Birkenhead and back behind 73035 and 73026 respectively. Clun worked her special from Didcot to here and then back to Birmingham Snow Hill whilst Pendennis took over at Didcot and returned her special back there from Chester. It was hydraulic power with a Hymek and a Western that were used for both legs out and back from Paddington. **Strathwood Library Collection & Tony Butcher**

As we have seen already a number of locomotives were repainted with their traditional style of numbering on the bufferbeams in true Great Western flair. Another of these to catch our eye was 1011 County of Chester, with a special near Abbotswood Junction on 20 September 1964 to bid farewell to the County Class. It ran out and back from Birmingham Snow Hill to Swindon on a circular route, out via Gloucester and Kemble, the return back via Didcot, Oxford and Leamington Spa. *Strathwood Library Collection*

Bristol Shiftwork

Chocolate and cream stock for the Devonian but this time a filthy Jubilee 45667 Jellicoe at Bristol Temple Meads in 1962. This service was a bit of misnomer for many years, because outside of the summer months the service did not go Devon at all, instead it ran between Bradford and Bristol. Only extended to Torquay and Paignton in the warmer months for the benefit of holidaymakers. *Gerald Peacock*

Armed with a powerful flash gun our intrepid cameraman captured a number of views at Bristol Temple Meads after dark, as here with 45658 Keyes on 1 August 1964 with the night mail. **Dave Down**

Page opposite: Several weeks later on 25 September, it befell 6820 Kingstone Grange to act as the standby locomotive should it be needed at Temple Meads, and for any shunting requirements during the shift. **Dave Down**

Back to August 1964, and Black Five 45417 has paused at Temple Meads long enough to grab another shot with the flash. Then again the same year on 26 September it is the turn of Britannia 70001 Lord Hurcomb with what looks like the same crew rostered for this turn. *Both Dave Down*

The Temple Meads station pilot on 18 August 1964 was Class 4F, 44135 supplied from Bristol's Barrow Road shed in the last months of its thirty-nine years of service, the crew look pretty relaxed as they await instructions from control. **Dave Down**

Page opposite: We close our night shift at the city's St.Phillips Marsh shed in 1962, with some disposal and preparation duties now that the sun has come up again. With 1361 Class 0-6-0ST, 1365 taking on water this morning, it would be the last one of her class to be scrapped, in September 1963. **Gerald Peacock**

Page left: Just in case their tenders could find further use they have been all been removed from this line up on death row at Swindon in the summer of 1962. The line includes large Prairie 6157 which had been withdrawn in May and would perish here by that September. It should also be noted many of the condemned still carry their name and numberplates. *John Gill*

Awaiting its destiny in front of the cutting staff on 18 October 1959 just a few weeks after being withdrawn was 7743. It would soon be be moved into position from the sidings adjoining the gas works however, as it was cut up in January 1960. *Frank Hornby*

The reign of 6025 King Henry III was soon to end at Swindon in March 1964. For it had been withdrawn from service in December 1962, after languishing on death row the final disposal would taken place two months after this shot was taken. *Late Norman Browne/Strathwood Library Collection*

Fellow enthusiasts take the numbers of what they can as they pass along the lines in Swindon's scrapping area on 12 August 1962. This task is made easier on 5682 as the smokebox numberplate has yet to be removed. One cannot but wonder whether this now valuable souvenir survived to fall into the hands of collectors? *Frank Hornby*

Again a small party are making their way this time around the gas works sidings in search of what awaits entry to the works. Such as 1652 on 26 March 1961, the lightweight 1600 Class Pannier had been withdrawn in January 1960, ironically it had been built here at Swindon Works just five years beforehand in December 1954, it would perish here too in July 1961. *Strathwood Library Collection*

Page opposite: Conversely the story of the Churchward designed 2818, would read that it was built here at Swindon Works in December 1905, giving valuable service until withdrawn in October 1963. It was then kept in the yard alongside less fortunate classmates such as 3855 as here on 3 April 1965. Further irony was that it would then be the works of the Southern Region at Eastleigh that would be given the task of restoring 2818 as part of The National Collection in 1966. *Edward Dorricott*

Page left: The partly cut boilers from at least five pannier tanks were also to be found on that same visit to Swindon Works on 3 April 1965, the clever use of a redundant bridge allowing the boilers to be supported whilst they are cut up. *Edward Dorricott*

Enthusiasts are here again on 24 July 1964 inspecting the locomotives awaiting disposal, including 9420 at the front of the line, she would be gone within days now, her remains no doubt sent to the hungry steel furnaces of South Wales for re-use. *Frank Hornby*

Preservation Movements

Page left: Happily from all this carnage of the steam fleet, some examples were chosen to survive for preservation. Such as the Great Western Society's 1466, seen shuffling alongside the mainline at Cholsey on 21 September 1968. **Strathwood Library Collection**

In pretty much original condition and restored for display in the Science Museum was 4073 Caerphilly Castle, awaiting transfer to Kensington by Pickfords low loaders waits inside the carriage sheds at Old Oak Common in June 1961, the loading took place at Park Royal. **Strathwood Library Collection**

Page left: Back to the activities of the Great Western Society once more, to enjoy 7808 Cookham Manor at an estimated 80mph on the approaches to West Ruislip on 17 September 1966. The tour was from Birmingham Snow Hill and back to allow the Manor to appear at the Open Day being held at Taplow. *Aldo Delicata*

Now preserved and safe from the cutters, was the resplendant externally at least 4079 Pendennis Castle. Seen coming off shed at Southall during 1965 complete with Great Western lettering once more. The controversial export to West Australia was yet to come! *Strathwood Library Collection*

The task of delivering this pairing of 3205 and 4555 to the Dart Valley Railway at Totnes was undertaken in connection with a special from Paddington, using 4079 Pendennis Castle and Warship D841 Roebuck. We see the duo heading for Totnes from Exeter St. Davids on 2 October 1965. *Dave Down*

Page opposite: An early Great Western preservation candidate was 3440 City of Truro storming through Theale on its way to Bristol via Trowbridge, having taken over this tour from 30453 King Arthur at Reading General on 28 April 1957. *Aldo Delicata*

Cambrian Adventures

The overall roof at Shrewsbury was already in the process of being dismantled when this shot of 1025 County of Radnor was recorded in May 1962. It looks as though there are a good number of spotters on hand as its the Whitsun holidays. A few weeks beforehand the BRCW built prototype D0260 Lion was visiting here on trials, just as 6964 Thornbridge Hall was bringing the Cambrian Coast Express through the town. ***Both: Strathwood Library Collection***

A reasonably clean 2859 being still fresh from its last works visit, was seen making its way around the yards at Shrewsbury in 1962 between freight workings.
Strathwood Library Collection

Page opposite: One of the self weighing tenders is attached to Black Five 45298, as it gets away from Llantwythd Wells with a Shrewsbury service on a glorious 13 July 1963.
Peter Simmonds

Also noted the same sunny day at Llantwythd Wells with a Swansea train was 73095. *Peter Simmonds*

One of the many Cambrian Coast regulars was 7819 Hinton Manor at Oswestry in 1963. *Strathwood Library Collection*

Taken the same day was this shot of the smartened up 7803 Barcote Manor again at Oswestry. **Strathwood Library Collection**

Page opposite: The meeting of the Talyllyn line with Edward Thomas at the bufferstops compares with the standard gauge bulk of 75009 waiting in the exchange siding in August 1966 at Towyn. **Edward Dorricott**

Page left: Another stop off at Oswestry next in 1963 to await the departure shortly of 7812 Erlestoke Manor. **Strathwood Library Collection**

It looks like a good number of passengers have just alighted from the Gobowen train at Oswestry that 1458 has just propelled in on 20 July 1963. **Peter Simmonds**

Page left: Taken on the same trip on 20 July 1963, our cameraman is hurried along as they want to get Standard 3MT 82031 back on its way to Carmarthen from Tregavron. *Peter Simmonds*

Passengers only just out number the platform staff at Dolgellau as Standard Class 4MT 75006 arrives in 1963. ***Strathwood Library Collection***

The summer of 1963 was a fabulous time to explore the Cambrian section, as we see Standard 4MT 80105 piloting 7820 Dinmore Manor away from Machynlleth with the Shrewsbury bound Cambrian Coast Express on 20 July. Whilst our cameraman was on hand again the same day to record 7810 Draycott Manor picking up the staff at Lampeter whilst in charge of a Carmarthan train. *Both: Peter Simmonds*

Page left: The evening mail train was the duty of 7810 Draycott Manor two months later in September the same year at Dovey Junction, as the shadows lengthen with today's sunset approaching. *Edward Dorricott*

More activity at Dovey Junction two years beforehand as 7827 Lydham Manor awaits onward movement whilst Standard Class 3MT, 82021 starts to blow at her safety valves on the other line. ***Strathwood Library Collection***

The Vale of Rheidol narrow guage trio are all picked up at Aberystwyth. First of all with 7 Owain Glyndwr in 1956, then two years later for 8 Llywelyn, and finally on 8 June 1963 to bag 9 Prince of Wales being coaled at the original narrow gauge shed. **Strathwood Library Collection & Frank Hornby**

In this pleasant view across Barmouth's waterfront, what looks like a Dukedog gets away in 1956. During the 1950s the deliveries of both Ivatt and Riddles 2MT Moguls sent the Dukedogs to the scrapmen, on the lightly laid Cambrian section where we meet 46446 of the Ivatt design in 1963. *Both: Strathwood Library Collection*

Specials were run in the early days for members to travel to the Ffestiniog Railway Society's AGM. These involved pairs of Dukedogs initially, however by the time of the 1960 meeting on 30 April they were almost extinct. As a result 7827 Lydham Manor was provided as the pilot to 9021 where the pair stopped for water at Barmouth. The duo took over at Ruabon for the run to Minffordd and back, whilst 1019 County of Merioneth had been requested as the Ffestiniog Railway is situated in what was then the namesake's county, in the event the train was taken by 1021 County of Montgomery for the Paddington to Ruabon and return legs. *Craig McBrine Collection*

Interlopers

Page left: We take our leave of the Cambrian section, with Standard Class 4MT 75012 passing one of the tank engine versions of the same power classification at Machynlleth in 1964. *Strathwood Library Collection*

Another Ian Allan publishing arranged special on 1 September 1964, brought 46245 City of London to Paddington for a run to allow spotters to visit Crewe Works, going out via Birmingham Snow Hill and Shrewsbury. *Strathwood Library Collection*

Page left: We have seen Western Region specials starting from the Southern Region, how about one going the other way instead? On 12 October 1958, we find Class E1, 31019 ready to depart Paddington for Kent! *Strathwood Library Collection*

Or perhaps a tender first freight working for nicely presented 46101 Royal Scots Grey, near Old Oak Common on 22 October 1962. *Strathwood Library Collection*

Page left: Final preparations are well in hand at 81C Southall for Class A4, 60007 Sir Nigel Gresley to make its return run to Manchester Exchange from Paddington on 23 October 1965, in charge of the Paddington Streamliner Railtour, raising funds for the A4 Preservation Society. *Strathwood Library Collection*

In the 1960s, Swindon Works carried out several light overhauls on Ivatt Class 4MTs such as 43047 seen awaiting the journey home to the London Midland Region outside 82C Swindon's running shed in August 1964, without a shedplate. *Late Norman Browne/Strathwood Library Collection*

Page left: Here's another Southern Region locomotive starting a tour from the Western Region, this time its Battle of Britain Pacific 34051 Winston Churchill leaving Banbury on 23 May 1965, having started the train from Birmingham Snow Hill, it was heading for the next changeover at Salisbury. *Strathwood Library Collection*

This time its 4472 Flying Scotsman approaching Kings Sutton with the Farnborough Flyer tour for the air show. Which it worked from Sheffield as far as Basingstoke where 34037 Clovelly was on hand. The tour was arranged by the famous A3's owner the late Alan Pegler for 12 September 1964. *Strathwood Library Collection*

On 24 June 1962 it was the turn of 30850 Lord Nelson to visit Swindon for a works and a shed visit for the Home Counties Railway Club. The opportunity was also taken to visit the newly opened Great Western Railway Museum which opened its doors two days beforehand. *Strathwood Library Collection*

Page opposite: No lining sadly, but at least a coat of fresh green paint for 4300 Class, 7340 on 28 May 1961. This locomotive had been originally numbered as 9318 when built at Swindon in April 1932, taking on this new number as 7340 in December 1957. *Frank Hornby*

Ex Works Swindon

The Great Western Railway built their 4200 Class 2-8-0T locomotives to the design of Churchward between 1910 and 1923. They were designed for short-haul coal trips from coal mines to ports in South Wales, working the heaviest coal trains through the Welsh valleys. The locomotives were built with large boilers and narrow side tanks; they were to have been designed to be capable of passing numerous water stops along their routes. However because of the class's heavy water consumption and limited tank capacity to feed such a large boiler they were nicknamed "Water Carts". Many of the lines in South Wales had sharp curves, to traverse these curves, the locomotives were constructed with side play in the trailing driving wheels and coupling rods, with spherical joints to allow for movement in any direction. The later build of 5205 Class were very similar although some were to be rebuilt in the form of 2-8-2Ts and classified as the 7200 Class. Standing outside Swindon's famous works ready for a return to traffic until it was withdrawn in October 1963 was 4257 on 8 February 1960. *Frank Hornby*

The plain and sometimes lined black liveries for the Prairie tank fleet had given way to the application of the more pleasing lined green as applied to 5182 outside the works in the sunshine on 20 September 1959. However this would not last, as the final overhauls for such engines were sending them back out in plain lined green, as we witness 6167 ready to go back into traffic on 11 May 1963 outside the works. *Both: Strathwood Library Collection*

There was a much higher standard of finish given to Standard Class 5MT 73093 on 8 March 1964 in lined black livery as it awaits re-uniting with its tender once, then testing can take place and the locomotive be signed back off the works into traffic once more. **Dave Down**

Page opposite: Final fettling needs to be completed on Standard Class 4MT 75008 by the works turntable in 1962, as the locomotive was destined for a return to traffic on the Western Region, Swindon's painters have gone to town on a splendid lined green livery instead. **Strathwood Library Collection**

Page left: For one of the Hawksworth designed 9400 Class the painters have left the copper chimney cap polished, but have elected to paint the brass safety valve cowl black, as she awaits release again on 24 March 1963. *Frank Hornby*

Running in on one of the local stoppers was the trip of choice for many an ex-works 4-6-0 from Swindon, with 6007 King William III ready to follow this pattern during 1961 as it waits at Swindon station. *John Gill*

The temptation to take a look in the cab is there for one enthusiast at Swindon on 9 April 1961, as 4902 Aldenham Hall waits for release from the works. *Frank Hornby*

Page opposite: Both the North British built Warship D833 Panther which has arrived for light repairs and Standard Class 4MT 76037 will soon go back into service again after this visit on 12 June 1964. *Peter Coton*

When the building programme of British Railways steam locomotives ended with 92220 Evening Star in 1960, firstly it was the construction of last of the Warships, then a batch of Westerns and finally the wasteful D9500 series of 0-6-0s that shared the main workshops, with this Standard Class 9F and a Grange both in for overhauls. We all perhaps prefer to remember Swindon for ex-works lined green 4-6-0s such as 4914 Cranmore Hall at the nearby running shed in 1960 in front of a likewise magnificent Castle. *Strathwood Library Collection & Richard Icke*

Help To Preserve Our Railway Heritage

Strathwood not only publish books on our railway heritage but have also set up the Railway Photographic Preservation Association as a Charitable Trust to house an archive of images comprising over 200,000 photographic negatives and slides.

The archive was established to not only preserve the collections of over one hundred photographers both living and deceased, but to also make their work available to a younger audience for the future. To achieve this aim, we have begun an energetic programme to publish a considerable number of books. Allied to this we are making as many as possible of the photographs and slides we hold, available as copies to interested enthusiasts, individuals, societies and other publishers.

Many photographers have chosen Strathwood to care for their collections and to publish the best examples of their work for posterity.

If you have negatives or colour slides of transport subjects then we would like to hear from you. We purchase, accept on loan, or welcome donations of material to the archive. Photographers always receive recognition for their work when it is used by publishers (A N Other/Strathwood Library). To answer why so many images are just credited as Strathwood Library Collection in this volume, the reason is we do not know who the original photographer was. This is usually because their collection gets split up via auctions or collectors upon their death with no record of the late photographer for us to credit. Please do not let this happen to your collection. Make contact with us today to discuss what can be done to ensure your work is fully credited and recognised for both today and the future.

Please call us now if you would like to see your work in print, perhaps in a similar fashion to this publication. We also undertake publications to benefit charities and societies on behalf of our contributors. In addition we can store, and catalogue collections on behalf of clubs and societies by way of loan, thereby releasing such groups to concentrate on other aspects of their activities.

Strathwood,
9 Boswell Crescent,
Inverness,
IV2 3ET.

Telephone 01463 234004

Don't leave it any longer!
YOU can then see YOUR work in print.